The Beginner Prepper's Disaster Preparedness Guide

How To Stockpile Supplies, Establish Communication, Generate Your Own Power, and Bug Out of Dodge When Disaster Strikes

Benjamin Cooper

© 2024

Copyright © 2024

Disclaimer

Introduction

There's a widespread misconception about preppers out there.

Some envision them as paranoid individuals, perhaps even donning hazmat suits and holed up in doomsday bunkers, eagerly awaiting the next apocalypse. But that's not the reality for most preppers.

Sure, there might be a handful who fit that description, but they're a tiny fraction of the prepping community.

Prepperes, my friend, are just regular folks like you and me, who've taken proactive steps to prepare for potential emergencies. Being a prepper doesn't mean your whole life revolves around prepping. It's not about living in constant fear or sacrificing your current lifestyle.

In fact, becoming a prepper usually involves only moderate adjustments.

Outwardly, everything remains the same.

Internally, though, you're preparing to become more self-sufficient and ready for whatever comes your way. It's about finding a balance between hoping for the best and being prepared for the worst.

So, let's clear up some misconceptions and dive into what prepping is really about. Here's what this book covers:

- How to become a prepper

- Stockpiling and preserving food and water

- Establishing emergency communications

- Bugging out effectively

- How to defend your home

- Generating your own replenishable power

Are you ready to start? If so, let's dive right in.

Becoming A Prepper

Preppers aren't fueled by paranoia or irrational fear; they're driven by a sensible awareness of real-world risks and threats.

It's a fact often overlooked: humans have been prepping since ancient times. Even our nomadic ancestors fortified their encampments and stored provisions as a precaution against hardship.

Take the Great Depression of the 1930s, for example. While many were caught off guard by the economic collapse, some weathered the storm because they'd prepared in advance.

Preppers are simply proactive individuals who anticipate tough times and make plans accordingly—a practice as old as civilization itself. They're not alarmists, but they recognize the unpredictability of the world we live in.

Whether it's natural disasters like droughts, floods, or hurricanes, or larger-scale events such as pandemics or economic downturns, preppers understand the importance of readiness.

The financial crisis of 2008 and the COVID-19 pandemic of 2020 served as stark reminders of our vulnerability. Grocery store shelves emptied, and supply chains faltered, leaving many unprepared.

As a prepper, it's not about succumbing to fear but about embracing a mindset of preparedness. It's about being proactive, adaptable, and ready to face whatever challenges may come our way.

At the heart of the prepper's mindset lies proactivity—an ethos centered on taking proactive measures to enhance readiness for emergencies.

Key facets of this mindset include:

1. Risk Awareness: Preppers are acutely aware of potential risks and threats, spanning natural disasters, technological breakdowns, economic turmoil, or societal unrest. Rather than succumbing to paranoia, they pragmatically prepare for contingencies.

2. Self-Reliance: Central to prepping is the belief in self-reliance and self-sufficiency. Preppers prioritize personal responsibility for their safety, security, and well-being, striving to acquire essential skills, knowledge, and resources to meet basic needs independently.

3. Resourcefulness: Valuing resourcefulness, preppers maximize available resources, repurpose items, and find alternative uses for objects. They cultivate a mindset that optimizes everyday tools for various functions, enhancing their adaptability in adversity.

4. Continuous Learning: Preppers actively pursue education, training, and resources to bolster their capabilities in areas such as first aid, survival skills, and emergency communication. Their commitment to ongoing learning ensures readiness across diverse scenarios.

5. Long-Term Planning: Beyond immediate response, preppers engage in long-term planning to ensure sustainable preparedness. This involves developing comprehensive emergency plans, securing alternative energy and water sources, and anticipating prolonged disruptions.

6. Community Engagement: While emphasizing individual preparedness, preppers value mutual assistance and collaboration. They forge networks of like-minded individuals, families, and neighbors to exchange knowledge, share resources, and offer support during crises.

Speaking of community, this is arguably the most important part of all of becoming a prepper.

Having a supportive community of like-minded individuals in your area can be incredibly valuable. These are people you can build relationships with, share resources, and both learn from and teach one another.

Here's why it matters:

1 - Communities can pool their resources to tackle common challenges. If someone's running low on a particular item, others can chip in to replenish their supply.

2 - Joining forces with like-minded people is a top defense strategy in a grid-down disaster. Together, you can offer mutual support and protection, establishing perimeter defenses and emergency response protocols.

3 - Strong community bonds foster companionship and a sense of belonging, especially during tough times when individuals may feel isolated. By uniting, people can rely on each other for support and guidance.

To become a prepper, you will need to:

1 - Cultivate a can-do attitude and belief in your ability to overcome challenges.

2 - Emotional Regulation - Manage stress and anxiety through self-awareness and coping strategies like mindfulness and seeking support.

3 - Approach challenges with flexibility and creativity, breaking them down into manageable steps.

4 - Practice dealing with stressors to build resilience over time.

5 - Maintain connections with family, friends, and community members for emotional and practical support.

Incorporating these elements into your life will strengthen your ability to adapt and thrive in any situation.

Water

Water is top priority when it comes to disaster preparedness. There are three key aspects to consider:

1. Have a sufficient supply of water stored for emergencies when access to running water is cut off.

2. Establish a method to replenish your water stockpile independently.

3. Ensure you have the means to purify water and make it safe for consumption.

Each of these elements is essential for a comprehensive water preparedness plan. While we'll delve deeper into water storage and purification later, let's discuss some basic principles now.

Firstly, it's recommended to store at least two gallons of water per person per day. One gallon is for drinking, while the other is for personal hygiene and cleaning. Adhering to this allocation can be challenging, considering the average household uses 100 to 200 gallons daily. Regulating each family member to just two gallons per day may seem daunting, but it's crucial for preparedness.

To adapt to this regimen, consider practicing water rationing with your family for a week. This hands-on experience will help you adjust to the limited water supply and better prepare for potential emergencies.

To maintain the quality of stored water, it's crucial to familiarize yourself with various purification methods. Here are some highly effective techniques:

1. Boiling water is a simple and reliable method of purification. Bringing water to a rolling boil for at least one minute (or three minutes at higher altitudes) kills bacteria, viruses, and parasites present in the water.

2. Filtration involves passing water through a physical barrier or filter to remove contaminants like sediment, bacteria, and protozoa. Portable water filters with ceramic, activated carbon, or hollow fiber membranes are effective. Combining filtration with boiling ensures comprehensive purification.

3. Chlorine bleach or iodine tablets can disinfect water and kill harmful microorganisms. Adding the appropriate amount of unscented bleach or iodine to untreated water and allowing it to stand for the recommended contact time effectively purifies it.

4. UV water purifiers use ultraviolet light to sterilize water and deactivate microorganisms by disrupting their DNA. Compact and lightweight UV wands or pens can be easily immersed in water to kill viruses and bacteria.

5. Distillation involves heating water to create steam, which is then condensed back into liquid form to remove impurities. This method effectively eliminates contaminants, including heavy metals and organic compounds, by separating them from the water vapor.

In the average household, we go through a hefty amount of water daily—somewhere between 100 to 200 gallons. That water gets divvied up for all sorts of essential tasks like drinking, cleaning, and watering plants. But when the grid goes down, and taps run dry, you've got to be ready. That's where stocking up on water becomes crucial.

I suggest setting aside two gallons of water per person each day for disaster preparedness. One gallon should cover hydration needs, while the other can handle cooking, cleaning, and personal hygiene. While some folks might argue you can get by on just one gallon a day, trust me, sticking to two makes life a lot easier. Considering how much water we typically use, having that extra gallon provides some much-needed peace of mind.

Storing Water

Storing water is a breeze when you've got some trusty barrels set up outdoors, shaded from the sun. These barrels come in various sizes, from around fifty-five gallons to over a thousand gallons. But no matter the size, there are a few must-haves to consider:

First off, steer clear of any barrels containing Bisphenol A (BPA) or other nasty chemicals, especially if they'll be soaking up some sun. Opt for food-grade materials like polyethylene, high-density polyethylene (HDPE), or polypropylene to keep your water safe and sound.

Sunlight can wreak havoc on your water supply, so make sure those barrels have UV-resistant properties. Materials like polyethylene, polypropylene, stainless steel, or fiberglass should do the trick.

Last but not least, seal the deal with a tight-fitting lid or cap to keep out any unwanted guests—dust, debris, or worse. A secure seal ensures your water stays clean and ready for when you need it most.

Ensuring your water supply stays fresh and safe to drink requires some regular maintenance. Here's what you need to do:

- Plan on refreshing your water stash every six months to a year. Start by emptying out the containers completely, then refill them with fresh water. Give the containers a good scrub using mild dish soap and water, paying extra attention to corners and seams where gunk can lurk. Rinse them out thoroughly to banish any lingering soap suds, then sanitize them with a mixture of unscented bleach and water.

- Don't forget to label each container with the date it was filled. You can use a permanent marker on tape or labels that won't easily rub off, making it easy to keep track of how old your water is.

- Regular inspections are key to keeping your water storage in top shape. Keep an eye out for any signs of damage, leaks, or contamination, and replace any containers showing wear and tear. Make sure those lids are sealed tight to keep out any unwanted hitchhikers.

- To prevent your water from turning into a bacteria breeding ground, remember to use the FIFO (First In, First Out) principle. That means drinking the oldest water first and cycling through your supply regularly.

- Always check for sediment buildup at the bottom of your containers and use a siphon or spigot to draw water from above the sediment line if needed. And don't just glance at the surface—keep an eye on those temperature fluctuations too. Store your water in a cool, dark spot away from direct sunlight to keep those pesky microorganisms at bay.

Remember, storing water is just one piece of the puzzle. Knowing how to purify any water you collect is equally important, because drinking contaminated water can do more harm than good.

Boiling Water – Making It Safe To Drink

Boiling water is a tried-and-true method for purifying water, as it effectively eliminates disease-causing organisms like viruses, bacteria, and parasites by subjecting them to high temperatures. Even in cloudy or murky water, boiling can eradicate bacteria, although it doesn't remove visible sediment. To ensure thorough purification, I recommend combining boiling with filtering.

The process of boiling water is straightforward: bring the filtered water to a rolling boil for 1 minute (or 3 minutes at elevations above 6,500 feet). Then allow the boiled water to cool.

For convenience, I always keep a metal cup in both my bug out bag and car, along with a fire starter, ensuring I can boil water whenever needed.

Another effective method for purifying water is distillation, which involves converting water from liquid to vapor and back to liquid to remove contaminants. This process effectively eliminates bacteria, microorganisms, and various impurities from the water.

Filtering Water

While water filters all work on the same basic principle of using filtration media to make water safe to drink, there are several different types to choose from:

KDF Filters: Made mainly of zinc and copper, KDF filters are great for reducing heavy metals like iron, chlorine, bacteria, and algae from warm water. They're also budget-friendly.

Activated Carbon Filters: These filters, made from organic materials high in carbon, such as wood or coal, are excellent at absorbing organic compounds, chlorine, and certain chemicals. They're perfect for improving taste and odor, as well as reducing chlorine levels.

Polypropylene Water Filters: Crafted from synthetic polypropylene, these filters specialize in mechanical filtration, removing sediment, particles, and larger impurities from water.

Reverse Osmosis Filters: Featuring a semipermeable membrane, these filters allow water molecules to pass through while blocking larger contaminants like salts, heavy metals, and microorganisms. They're top-notch for comprehensive purification.

For a reliable water purification solution, consider investing in a large family-sized water filter to ensure all your water is safe to drink. Additionally, you can use another purification method to further eliminate any contaminants the filter might have missed.

Rainwater Harvesting

Rainwater harvesting is a traditional method of water collection that has been practiced for centuries, offering a softer alternative to tap water due to its lack of calcium, chlorine, and minerals. However, rainwater can still harbor pollutants from the atmosphere, necessitating purification before consumption.

It's essential to adhere to the golden rule: always purify harvested water before drinking it.

Understanding the potential volume of rainwater you can collect is key. You can determine this by using a simple equation:

1 inch of rain × 1 square foot = 0.62 gallons

For instance, on a typical thousand square foot roof, one inch of rainfall yields approximately 620 gallons of water.

To accurately estimate rainwater collection, start by determining the average annual precipitation in your region. Then, multiply this figure by the square footage available for collection using the provided formula.

The simplest rainwater harvesting method involves placing a water barrel at the base of a gutter downspout to catch runoff from the roof. Follow these steps for a successful setup:

1. Ensure your roof and gutters effectively channel rainwater to the collection system.
2. Use a food-grade polyester storage tank or barrel to capture rainwater safely.
3. Install a screen filter to prevent large debris from entering the collection system, especially in gutters prone to buildup.
4. Include an overflow drainage spout near the top of the barrel to prevent overflow, and connect it to another barrel to prevent waste.
5. Implement a filtration and purification system to guarantee the water's safety for consumption.
6. Utilize a water pump to extract water from the barrel for various applications.

Even in apartments or condos, you can employ makeshift methods like tarps or buckets to collect rainwater. However, remember that rainwater harvesting relies on rainfall for effectiveness.

Atmospheric Water Generators

If you're facing challenges with accessing water through traditional methods like well digging or rainwater harvesting, an atmospheric water generator (AWG) could be the solution you're looking for.

AWGs are devices designed to extract water from the air through condensation, providing a sustainable source of clean drinking water. These devices typically include filtration and purification systems to ensure the water is safe for consumption.

Consider using an AWG as a backup to your existing water supply system or as a primary method, especially if you live in an apartment or condo where traditional water harvesting methods aren't feasible.

Here's how AWGs work:

1. They draw in air from the surrounding environment using a fan or compressor.
2. The air is cooled below its dew point, causing water vapor to condense into liquid water droplets.
3. The condensed water droplets are collected on surfaces, such as coils or plates, within the AWG unit.
4. The collected water undergoes filtration and purification to remove impurities, ensuring its safety.
5. Purified water is stored in a reservoir within the AWG unit and can be dispensed on demand.

While AWGs may require a significant initial investment, the ongoing supply of clean drinking water they provide makes them a valuable long-term investment.

Digging Your Own Water Well

Water wells offer a dependable means of accessing groundwater, making them more reliable than rainwater harvesting methods.

There are two main approaches to establishing a water well: professional drilling or a do-it-yourself (DIY) method using a personal water well kit.

Professional well digging can be costly, with depths ranging from fifty to four hundred feet and costs potentially reaching up to $10,000, depending on the terrain.

A DIY water well offers a more economical option, requiring minimal investment and a bit more effort. Here's what you'll need:

- Auger
- Bore DIY Water Well Kit (including hand pump and 25 feet of PVC piping)
- Pea Gravel
- Pliers
- Saw
- Pipe Wrenches
- PVC primer
- Cordage
- Cap and Screen Assembly
- Drill Pipe
- Cement and Water Mixture

Follow these basic steps to build your DIY water well:

1. Select a suitable location, ideally based on professional inspection to confirm groundwater presence.
2. Use the auger to excavate the hole, aiming for a depth of around 25 feet to reach the phreatic zone.
3. Install the screen assembly at the bottom of the well for water filtration.
4. Lower the PVC pipe into the hole, ensuring the screen assembly is positioned at the bottom.
5. Fill the space around the PVC pipe with pea gravel for stability.
6. Insert the water pump into the PVC pipe, flushing out any muddy water.
7. Install the cap assembly and pump handle to complete the setup.

With these steps completed, your DIY water well is ready to provide you with a reliable source of water.

Food

The principles of preparing for food storage mirror those of water storage: accumulate a sufficient quantity, learn preservation techniques, and establish a means of replenishment.

While I'll delve into replenishing food supplies in a subsequent chapter, let's focus now on storing and preserving food, along with meal planning.

Preservation Method #1 – Pressure Canning

Pressure canning is the preferred method for preserving low-acid foods like meats and vegetables due to its ability to achieve higher temperatures necessary for effective bacteria elimination.

Materials Needed:

- Pressure canner
- Canning jars with lids and bands
- Jar lifter
- Lid lifter
- Clean towels
- Saucepan
- Spatula
- Canning funnel

Procedure:
1. Wash and sterilize the jars, lids, and bands.
2. Fill the jars with the desired food, removing air bubbles with a spatula.
3. Wipe the jar rims clean and seal with lids and bands.
4. Load the jars onto the pressure canner rack following the manufacturer's instructions.
5. Secure the canner lid and allow steam to vent for 10 minutes.
6. Close the vent and bring the canner to the recommended pressure.
7. Process the jars for the specified time based on the food being canned.
8. Allow the canner to cool naturally, then use a lifter to remove the jars and place them on a towel.
9. After 12 to 24 hours, check the lids for proper sealing.

Preservation Method #2 – Water Bath Canning

Water bath canning involves submerging food jars entirely in boiling water for a specified duration. To perform water bath canning, you'll need a water bath canner with a rack to hold the jars apart and ensure they are fully submerged.

Materials Needed:

- Water Bath Canner with Rack
- Saucepan
- Spatula
- Canning Funnel
- Lid Lifter
- Canning Jars (with lids and bands for each jar)
- Jar Lifter
- Towels

Procedure:

1. Thoroughly wash and sterilize the jars, lids, and bands. Boil the jars for 10 minutes and keep the lids and bands in hot water.
2. Use a jar lifter to remove the jars from boiling water and fill them with food, utilizing a canning funnel for easier filling.
3. Remove any air bubbles by gently mixing the food in the jar with a spatula.
4. Wipe the jar rims with a clean towel to ensure they are free from debris.
5. Place the lids over the jars and tightly secure them with the bands.
6. Arrange the jars on the rack inside the water bath canner pot, ensuring they are submerged by 1-2 inches of water.
7. Boil the water according to the recipe instructions for the specific food being canned.
8. Once done, use a jar lifter to remove the jars and place them on a clean towel to cool.
9. After 12-24 hours, check the lids for sealing by pressing down on the center. If it remains depressed, the jar is sealed.

Note that water bath canning is suitable for preserving high-acid foods, while low-acid foods should be pressure canned instead.

Preservation Method #3 – Freezing

Freezing is one of the most common methods of food preservation, and chances are, if you have a freezer at home, you're already using it! It's popular because it's versatile and can effectively store a wide range of foods, including meats, fruits, vegetables, baked goods, and dairy products, keeping them fresh for months or even years.

However, in the event of a natural disaster or an electromagnetic pulse (EMP) attack causing a power outage, your freezer's ability to function will be compromised. A fully loaded freezer can only maintain a safe frozen temperature for up to 48 hours after a power outage.

To prepare for such situations, it's essential to have a plan in place. Keep multiple large coolers and ice packs readily available for emergencies. When the power goes out, leave the food in the freezer for the initial 48 hours.

Afterward, transfer the frozen foods to a cooler filled with ice. If the cooler is well-insulated, it can keep the food preserved for up to a week. Another option is to invest in a solar-powered freezer, which operates using power generated by solar panels rather than relying on the power grid.

Preservation Method #4 – Vacuum Sealing

Vacuum packaging is a method where air is extracted from the packaging material, creating a vacuum-sealed environment around the food. This process prevents the growth of bacteria, molds, and other spoilage microorganisms by removing oxygen, which they need to survive.

To vacuum package food, you'll need a vacuum sealer machine. This device removes air from specially designed vacuum-seal bags or containers and then seals them shut with heat. It's a highly effective method for preserving various perishable foods, including meats, vegetables, fruits, grains, and even prepared meals.

Preservation Method #5 – Drying

Drying foods is one of the oldest methods of food preservation. It's a straightforward process: remove moisture from food to extend its shelf life.

Here are a few methods you can try:

Sun Drying: An ancient method, sun drying involves placing food directly in sunlight to let natural evaporation occur. It works best in hot, dry climates and is perfect for drying fruits, herbs, and some vegetables.

Air Drying: This method is as simple as it sounds. Just leave your food in an area with good airflow to let the water evaporate naturally. It's great for herbs and small batches of fruits and veggies, especially those with low water content.

Oven Drying: If you have a kitchen, you can use your oven to dehydrate food. Simply spread out fruits, vegetables, or meat on baking sheets and dry them out at low temperatures.

Removing moisture from your foods is just the beginning of the preservation process. After dehydration, you'll need to take a few more steps to ensure your food stays fresh:

Conditioning: This step involves equalizing the moisture content in dehydrated foods to prevent spoilage. Let the dehydrated foods cool on trays before transferring them to a container filled two-thirds of the way. Seal the container and shake it vigorously once daily for ten days, monitoring for condensation or signs of spoilage.

Packaging: Once conditioned, package the food to extend its shelf life. I recommend using food-storage bags with airtight seals or glass jars. Package foods in serving amounts to minimize moisture absorption once opened.

Storage: Store the packaged dehydrated food in a cool, dark location indoors, such as a cellar or basement, ideally around 60 degrees Fahrenheit. This helps maximize shelf life.

Just be sure to avoid keeping the packaged food in areas prone to temperature fluctuations or exposure to sunlight, as this can compromise its quality over time.

Storing Food

The foundation of your food storage should comprise non-perishable items that can be stored at room temperature. These include:

Canned goods, such as:
- Canned vegetables
- Canned fruits
- Canned meats
- Canned soups and stews

Dried foods with removed moisture, including:
- Beans and legumes
- Fruits
- Pasta
- Rice

Nuts and Seeds, such as:
- Almonds, walnuts, peanuts
- Sunflower seeds, pumpkin seeds, chia seeds
- Nut butters like peanut butter and almond butter

The fundamental principle of food preparation is that your pantry should be tailored to suit the needs of you and your family. While water storage is relatively straightforward—simply store plenty of clean and purified water—food storage is more nuanced due to the variety of factors involved and the range of foods to consider:

- Quantity: The amount of food you store should correspond to the size of your household. Larger families will naturally require more food storage compared to smaller households or individuals living alone.

- Preferences: Consider the food preferences of your family members, as long as the chosen foods are non-perishable or can be safely stored for extended periods. Variety is key—there's no need to limit yourself to a diet of beans and rice.

- Versatility: Opt for versatile foods that cover nutritional needs and can be used in various meal preparations. Alongside staples like beans and rice, incorporate canned meats, vegetables, and fruits to diversify your options.

- Allergies and Dietary Restrictions: Take into account any allergies or dietary restrictions within your family and avoid storing foods that could trigger allergic reactions.

- Expiration Dates: Implement a system to track expiration dates and rotate food items before they expire. Consider using a physical spreadsheet to monitor stored foods, quantities, and expiration dates effectively.

By considering these factors and tailoring your food storage approach accordingly, you can ensure that your pantry is well-equipped to sustain you and your family during uncertain times.

Energy

In this chapter, we'll dive into the top three ways that you can generate your own renewable energy on your property:

Wind Power

Wind power can be a valuable source of renewable energy, and setting up your own wind turbine is a great way to harness it. Here's how it works:

Wind turbines consist of a tower and blades. As the wind blows, the blades rotate, and this rotational motion is converted into electrical energy by a connected generator. This electricity can then power your household appliances and devices.

Before installing a wind turbine, it's essential to analyze your local wind patterns to ensure sufficient wind on your property.

Once you've confirmed suitable wind conditions, you can begin building your own wind turbine. Here's what you'll need:

- PVC pipes for turbine blades
- Charge controller
- Generator motor
- Base
- Wires

Here are the steps to build your wind turbine:

1. Cut the PVC pipes into blade shapes of equal length and size.
2. Attach the blades to a central hub or base to form the turbine structure.
3. Build or obtain a tower to elevate the turbine for better access to higher wind speeds.
4. Mount the generator motor at the top of the tower and connect it to the turbine blades.
5. Install a charge controller to regulate the electricity generated and protect connected batteries or devices.
6. Secure the turbine and tower onto a stable base, anchoring it firmly to the ground.
7. Connect the turbine to a battery bank or electrical system using appropriate wiring.
8. Test the turbine's functionality in an open area with consistent wind flow.
9. Position the turbine in an area with unobstructed wind flow, ideally at a higher altitude.

Additionally, seeking advice from someone already living off-grid can provide valuable insights into setting up your own power systems. They may even be willing to show you their process firsthand.

Water Power

In a typical hydroelectric setup, water is sourced from a river or dam and directed through turbines, which are connected to generators. The kinetic force of the moving water causes the turbines to rotate, converting this kinetic energy into mechanical energy. Subsequently, the mechanical energy is transformed into electrical energy by the generators, generating electricity suitable for various applications.

If your property features a stream of running water, you may have the potential to install a small-scale hydroelectric system modeled after the above to provide power and electricity to your home and property.

What makes hydropower appealing compared to solar and wind power is its predictability. Unlike sunlight or wind, the flow of water in a stream is consistent, providing a reliable source of energy.

The downside is the requirement of having a running stream of water on your property. However, if your property does have running water, you're in luck. Here's what you'll need:

- DC water pump
- Flow control system
- Mounting brackets
- Battery or energy storage system
- Wiring and electrical components
- Plastic or PVC piping
- Generator or alternator
- Pressure gauge
- Valves

Here's the basic process for setting up your hydroelectric system:

1. Evaluate the flow rate of your stream and select a location with consistent and robust water flow for steady power generation.
2. Submerge the DC water pump in the stream and connect it to plastic or PVC piping to convey water from the stream to the generator.
3. Implement valves and a flow control system to regulate water flow, optimizing energy production and safeguarding the system from fluctuations.
4. Connect the generator or alternator to the water pump, ensuring proper alignment, and secure mounting brackets for stability.
5. Install a pressure gauge to monitor water pressure, aiding in system management.
6. Connect the generator to a battery or energy storage system, enabling energy storage during peak production for a continuous power supply.
7. Incorporate necessary electrical components like switches and fuses to regulate power output and protect the system.

Solar Power

Solar power is an increasingly popular option for renewable energy, and setting up your own solar generator can be a rewarding project. Here's how it works:

Solar panels, made of photovoltaic (PV) cells, convert sunlight into electricity through the photovoltaic effect. This produces direct current (DC) electricity, which is then converted into usable alternating current (AC) electricity for household appliances using an inverter.

To create your own solar generator, you'll need:

- Solar panel
- Deep cycle battery
- Charge controller
- Power inverter
- DC to AC adapter
- Battery box
- Wires and connectors
- Insulated electrical tape

Here are the steps to set it up:

1. Choose a solar panel size based on your energy needs. A 50W panel is suitable for small applications.
2. Select a 12V deep-cycle battery suitable for solar use and your power requirements.
3. Use a charge controller to regulate voltage and prevent overcharging of the battery.
4. Place the deep cycle battery in a protective box for safety.
5. Connect the solar panel to the charge controller using appropriate wires and connectors.
6. Connect the charge controller to the battery, ensuring correct polarity.
7. Connect the power inverter to the battery to convert DC to AC electricity.
8. If you need DC outlets, install adapters for direct charging.
9. Use a multimeter to verify voltage and check all connections.
10. Securely place all components in the battery box.
11. Position the solar panel in sunlight and test the generator to ensure proper charging and power supply.

With your solar generator set up, you'll be able to harness clean and renewable solar energy to power your household appliances or charge your devices.

Security

Securing both your home and property is paramount. Unfortunately, many homes today lack sufficient defenses and are vulnerable to break-ins. This vulnerability contributes to the prevalence of burglaries, a trend that may worsen in a grid-down disaster scenario when traditional supply chains are disrupted, and desperation increases.

It's crucial to dispel the notion that "My home will never be broken into." Too often, victims of burglaries had this belief before the incidents occurred. Therefore, taking proactive measures now to enhance the defensibility of your home is imperative. Consider your home as your personal fortress. Just as people fortified castles in the past to defend against outside assaults, you should aim to make your home equally difficult to breach.

Bolstering Your Home and Property's Security

To bolster your home's security and deter break-ins, consider the following steps:

- Reinforce all exterior doors with steel construction to enhance durability and resistance to forced entry. Steel doors provide a formidable barrier against potential intruders wielding tools like axes or sledgehammers.

- Strengthen windows with acrylic glass, a resilient material that adds an additional layer of protection against break-ins. Acrylic glass enhances security without compromising the aesthetic appeal of your home.

- Upgrade standard locks and hinges to heavy-duty alternatives that offer increased strength and resilience. Combined with steel doors, these components significantly elevate the security of your home.

By reinforcing the most vulnerable entry points into your home, such as doors and windows, these measures automatically enhance your home's defensibility and deter potential intruders.

Securing your property is equally important. Consider investing in stakes and barbed wire to establish a perimeter around your property when the grid goes down.

While a barbed wire fence may not align with your everyday aesthetic preferences, it can serve as an effective deterrent after a disaster. The primary goal is to keep potential threats away from your home.

Setting up two or three layers of barbed wire fencing, if feasible, can further enhance security and deterrence. The appearance of a formidable barrier sends a clear message to would-be intruders that your property is not an easy target.

During a grid-down disaster, looters often target vulnerable properties. A visible barbed wire fence signals to potential intruders that breaking in will not be easy and may encourage them to seek easier targets elsewhere. Ultimately, the goal is to keep your property secure and minimize the risk of intrusion.

Defense: Keeping the Attackers At Bay

Sure, here's a reorganized version:

- The first line of defense is arming yourself. Ensure you have access to firearms and non-lethal options for self-defense.

- Set up a perimeter defense using methods like barbed wire fencing and alarm systems to deter intruders from breaching your property.

- Fortify your windows with sandbags to provide essential cover during a confrontation.

- Mislead intruders by creating deceptive cover to lure them into exposing themselves while you maintain a tactical advantage.

- Strategically place nailboards around your property or behind doors to hinder aggressors and buy yourself valuable time.

- Dig concealed pits lined with sharp stakes to immobilize or injure attackers and thwart their advance.

Alarm System

Repurposing materials like tin or aluminum cans, bells, string or wire, and stakes, you can easily set up this alarm system to enhance security around your property. Here's how:

1. Identify key entry points or paths around your property where you want to set up the alarm system. If feasible, create a complete perimeter around your property.

2. Stretch a string or wire across the chosen area, securing the ends to stakes to keep them stable.

3. Attach tin or aluminum cans to the string at regular intervals along its length.

4. Fill the cans with pebbles or small rocks. These will serve as the alarm mechanism.

5. When an intruder trips over the string, the movement will cause the pebbles in the cans to rattle, alerting you to their presence.

6. Ensure that the string is set up at a relatively low height, such as knee height or lower. This makes it less likely for intruders to notice and attempt to step over it, increasing the effectiveness of the alarm system.

Communications

In a post-grid down world, one of the most significant shifts we'll experience is in how we connect with each other.

These days, reaching out is as easy as a tap or a click - whether it's a call, a text, an email, or a quick message on our favorite social media platform. But when the grid goes down, our electronic lifelines will go silent. No more cell service, no more internet - and suddenly, our go-to communication methods become obsolete.

So, how do you stay connected when your usual channels are cut off? It's not just about reaching across the country; even your neighbors a few miles away might as well be worlds apart.

The answer lies in alternative communication devices - and knowing how to use them is key.

Emergency Radios – Two Way

Often referred to as two-way radios, walkie-talkies offer a simple and effective communication solution for short-range interactions. With the press of a push-to-talk button, users can instantly communicate with others tuned into the same frequency. While they excel in straightforward one-on-one conversations, it's important to note that they are limited to small areas compared to other communication options available.

There's a neat trick you can pull off to maximize the range of your two-way radios, especially if you've got a bunch of people involved.

Typically, the range of most two-way radios is around five to six miles, but some fancier models claim they can reach up to twenty or even thirty miles.

Here's how you can stretch that range: Let's say Person A has a radio and chats with Person B, who's a good thirty miles away. Then, Person B relays the message to Person C, who's another thirty miles away. You can keep this relay going as long as you've got folks within range and willing to pass the message along. Pretty neat, huh?

Emergency Radios – CB

Citizens Band (CB) radios work within a specific range of 40 channels within the 27 MHz frequency band. These radios provide a dependable way to communicate over short to medium distances, operating independently of cell networks or the internet.

What sets CB radios apart is their versatility and portability. They come in mobile and handheld versions, easily fitting into vehicles or carried along wherever you go.

Emergency Radios – HAM

HAM radios, also known as amateur radios, are popular among preppers who establish local HAM networks within their communities to share information, updates, and mutual assistance.

These radios provide access to designated emergency frequencies and offer various communication options, including voice, data, and Morse code, across different HAM bands. While operating a HAM radio requires some technical knowledge, obtaining a license will teach you how to use them. The licensing process ensures understanding of regulations, operating procedures, and radio electronics. Prospective operators must pass a licensing exam administered by the relevant regulatory body in their country or jurisdiction.

T are three main FCC licenses for HAM radio operators:

1. Technician: This entry-level license requires passing a 35-question multiple-choice exam.
2. General: To obtain a General license, you must pass a similar multiple-choice exam along with a 5-word-per-minute Morse code test.
3. Amateur Extra: This highest-level license involves passing a 50-question multiple-choice exam.

Additionally, there are three primary types of HAM radios: base, mobile, and handheld. Base radios, the largest and most powerful, are typically stationary devices. Mobile radios are smaller and designed for vehicle mounting, while handheld radios are compact and portable, allowing for easy carrying.

Protecting Your Emergency Communication Devices From EMP Attacks and Solar Flares

A Faraday cage is like an electronic safe house, shielding your gadgets from the chaos of electromagnetic fields, especially during events like an EMP.

To set up your own Faraday cage, you'll need three key ingredients:

- Pick a sturdy metal container like a steel or aluminum trash can, ammo can, or metal filing cabinet. Make sure it's made of conductive material.

- Line the inside of your chosen container with insulating material such as cardboard, foam, or rubber. This layer keeps your devices from touching the metal, enhancing protection.

- Use conductive tape, aluminum foil, or metal mesh to seal the edges of the container. This prevents electromagnetic leaks and ensures your cage is a fortress against interference.

Here's how you can put it all together:

1. Clean the inside of your metal container thoroughly to remove any obstacles to its shielding abilities.

2. Cut your insulating material to fit the container's interior and line it along the bottom and sides. Cover every inch to keep your devices cozy.

3. Place your electronic gadgets inside the container, making sure they're spaced out to avoid touching metal surfaces.

4. Apply your chosen sealant around the container's edges, ensuring a tight closure. Overlap the material at corners for added security.

5. Before sealing the container shut, do a quick test. Pop a device inside and close the lid. If it loses signal, you're good to go. That means your cage is ready to fend off any electromagnetic mayhem that comes its way.

And that's it!

Bugging Out

We've covered a lot about preparing your home for disaster: stocking up on essentials, fortifying your defenses, living more self-sufficiently, and establishing emergency communication methods.

But there's another aspect to consider: evacuation. It's a real possibility that you may need to leave your home. Whether it's at the authorities' orders or because it's no longer safe, bugging out might be necessary. Natural disasters like earthquakes or hurricanes could force you to evacuate.

That's why, as a prepper, you always need to be ready to bug out. It should be part of your plans, and you should be prepared to leave at a moment's notice if needed.

Building A Bug Out Bag

Bug out bags rank among the most popular concepts in the prepping realm, and rightfully so. Essentially, a bug out bag is a backpack stuffed with survival essentials intended to sustain you and provide a degree of comfort during your journey to a safer bug out location. In essence, your bug out bag serves as a lifeline in case you need to evacuate from home.

No two bug out bags are identical, and I strongly discourage purchasing a pre-made bug out bag online. Instead, opt for buying a backpack and individual items separately. This approach ensures you're intimately familiar with your pack's contents, enhancing its effectiveness in an emergency.

When selecting a backpack for your bug out bag, consider the following criteria:

- Look for durability in materials like nylon, polyester, cordura, or ripstop fabrics to ensure your bag can withstand rugged conditions.

- Choose a bag made from water-resistant or waterproof materials to protect your gear from moisture and environmental elements.

- Opt for darker shades like black, brown, gray, dark green, or dark blue to blend in with your surroundings and avoid attracting unwanted attention.

- * Seek a backpack with one large compartment for bulkier items and smaller compartments for easy access to essentials like first aid supplies or fire-starting tools.

- Prioritize features like padded shoulder straps, adjustable waist belts, and back ventilation systems to ensure comfortable wear, especially during extended periods of use. Adjustability is key to accommodate different body sizes and minimize strain.

Then you can fill up your pack with the things you'll need to get you to your bug out location. You should customize your bag as you see fit, but I would suggest:

- Water (at least one gallon per person per day)
- Non-perishable food items (three-day supply per person)
- Clothing appropriate for various weather conditions
- Lightweight tent, tarp, or emergency shelter
- First aid kit (bandages, antiseptic wipes, medications)
- Essential tools (knife, multi-tool, axe, saw, duct tape)
- Fire starter kit (waterproof matches, lighters, fire starters)
- Flashlights, headlamps, or lanterns with extra batteries
- Map, compass, or GPS device for navigation
- Portable radio or hand-crank emergency radio
- Whistle, signaling mirror, or other communication devices
- Personal hygiene items (toilet paper, hand sanitizer, wet wipes)
- Copies of important documents (identification, insurance papers)
- Cash in small denominations
- Personal defense items (pepper spray, tactical flashlight)
- Entertainment and comfort items (books, playing cards, journal)

Assembling Your Family

Before you bug out, it's crucial to gather your family members together.

Set specific meeting points for you, your spouse, and your children in case of an emergency. Once you've reunited with your spouse, head to your children's locations next. If they're at school during the incident, designate their schools as meeting points and prioritize picking them up from there. If they're elsewhere, meet them wherever they are.

Keeping track of our children's whereabouts is key to our preparedness plan. Whether they're on a field trip, visiting friends, or out and about, knowing their plans lets us react quickly in an emergency. In the event of an EMP attack, my wife and I would travel on foot to reach our children.

Since electronic communication won't be an option post-EMP attack, having a solid plan in place is even more vital. To boost preparedness, consider creating physical contact cards for each family member with essential info like names, addresses, and emergency contacts.

Give these cards to everyone and encourage them to keep them in their wallets or pockets for easy access. Stress the importance of memorizing key contact details in case the cards are lost or unavailable.

Putting Your Bug Out Plan Into Action

Bugging out is typically riskier than bugging in. When you're bugged in at home during a disaster, you have access to your supplies, self-sufficiency measures, and the fortified walls of your home we discussed earlier.

But sometimes, bugging out is your only option. It means leaving your home and supplies behind, making you vulnerable on the road.

That's why a solid bug out plan is crucial. It should include a destination and multiple routes to get there safely.

A bug out plan isn't complete without a designated bug out location. This is where you'll head during an evacuation. Knowing exactly where you're going is crucial; aimlessly wandering around is the last thing you want to do.

The two most common bug out locations are:

1. Another property you own, like a bug out retreat.
2. The home of a friend or family member outside the danger zone.

Bug out retreats are often secluded, with limited access and surrounded by natural features for security and resources. Some preppers invest in secluded property and set up cabins or living structures there. If you plan to stay with a friend or family member, it's essential to confirm with them beforehand.

The golden rule of bugging out is to leave as early as possible. When a mass evacuation is underway, roads become congested, slowing travel to a crawl. If vehicles are disabled due to an EMP attack or solar flare, you'll find yourself navigating through throngs of evacuees on foot or by bicycle.

If feasible, make the decision to bug out early. While it's not always avoidable to evacuate with the crowd, anticipating untenable conditions allows you to act preemptively. For instance, if you're alerted to an approaching natural disaster, opting to bug out ahead of official orders can be prudent.

Once you've chosen your bug out location, map out multiple evacuation routes.

I recommend having at least three routes to your bug out location, with contingency plans to switch between them if needed. Should your primary route become blocked, a detour route leading to an alternative path can prove invaluable.

Practice driving these routes until they're ingrained in your memory. Don't solely rely on maps or GPS; physical familiarity with the terrain is key.

What Can We Conclude?

Becoming a prepper is fundamentally about self-reliance and achieving independence in everyday life, akin to traditional methods of providing for oneself and family. Despite the hurdles encountered along the journey, each obstacle overcome reinforces the sense of accomplishment derived from self-sufficiency. Knowing that my family and I can sustain ourselves, even in the face of societal disruptions or a collapse of the power grid, brings immense peace of mind.

If there are any specific takeaways from this book as we come to a close, it would be the following: Assess your risks by identifying potential threats and risks specific to your location and circumstances.

Develop a comprehensive emergency plan outlining actions before, during, and after a disaster. Stockpile essential supplies, including food, water, medical supplies, and hygiene products, aiming for at least a one-month supply. Learn how to filter and purify water and have means to replenish your water supply.

Master basic food preservation techniques and have means to replenish your food supply. Acquire first aid training, assemble a comprehensive first aid kit, and learn essential medical skills. Prioritize personal safety and property security with self-defense training and appropriate tools. Establish reliable communication channels and stay informed during emergencies. Incorporate renewable energy solutions and ensure access to electricity for essential devices.

Continued learning and engagement with the off-grid community provide valuable insights and support for those embarking on the journey. Cultivate a sense of fulfillment in reclaiming control over livelihood and knowing you'll be okay in times of crisis.

That's because... you will be okay.